Soul Shimmers

Awakening Your Spiritual Self

Gloria Chadwick

Mystical Mindscapes
Books to Enlighten and Empower

Soul Shimmers
Awakening Your Spiritual Self

Publisher's Cataloging-in-Publication Data

Chadwick, Gloria / ISBN 1-883717-83-3
Soul Shimmers: Awakening Your Spiritual Self
1. Dreams   2. Spirituality 3. Meditation   I. Title

Library of Congress Catalog Card Number: 99-70664

Published by Mystical Mindscapes
1908 Cambridge Court • Palatine, IL 60074

Cover Art by Kathy Beening

Printed in the United States of America
by Morris Publishing, Kearney, Nebraska

Books by Gloria Chadwick

Exploring Your Past Lives

Somewhere Over the Rainbow
A Soul's Journey Home

Images and Inner Journeys
Meditations and Visualizations

The Key to Self-Empowerment
Open the Magic Inside Your Mind

Happy Ways to Heal the Earth

Soul Shimmers
Awakening Your Spiritual Self

May this book remind you of your soul's
inner knowing, and be a way-shower
on your journey to spiritual awakening.

Once upon a dream ...

This book is dedicated to the philosopher.

Thanks for sharing your knowledge and for journeying with me on the rainbow path.

Contents

One

The Rainbow Path

I listened to the rain patter gently on the glass of the open window. Thinking that I should get up and close the window, I noticed that it was nearly dawn and the sun was beginning to rise. I thought this was curious — that the sun could be seen through the clouds.

I rose to close the window and looking up at the sky, I saw the most beautiful rainbow I've ever seen. It was *shimmering* in the light reflected from the sun, radiating sparkles of rainbow-colored light everywhere.

I wondered how a rainbow could appear in the sky when it was still raining and the sun wasn't fully above the horizon or clearly visible through the soft, misty clouds and decided that I must be dreaming.

"Follow your dream," the rainbow said.

If I was dreaming, I thought to myself, then maybe I could fly up into and through this magical, mystical rainbow to experience the awe and wonder and joy of it with every part of my being.

It sounded like a wonderful thing to do and I decided to follow this dream to see where the rainbow would lead me.

I had a feeling that if I could somehow get inside this rainbow, and if I totally involved all my senses in exploring and experiencing the rainbow with every part of my awareness — seeing, touching, smelling, tasting, and hearing the harmony of the colors — I could become the essence of the rainbow. Then maybe I'd be able to *feel* the energies of the colors vibrating all around me and through me, inside my heart, within my body and my mind, encircling my soul.

I wanted to feel the vibrations of the rainbow emanating from within my body — from within the center of my being, the very core of my soul — and radiating outward from myself. I wanted to become a rainbow of colors, vibrating and shimmering in a magical flow and radiance of energy, expanding both inward and outward.

If I could become the rainbow, then I could rise above the rainbow through the mist into the white light of the Universe, and I could become the essence of white light and feel the light vibrating in harmony with my soul, in tune with my spiritual essence.

I heard the voice whisper again in my mind, somewhere inside my dream. "Would you like to take a wonderful journey into a magical, mystical place where you can follow a rainbow path to open up the true reality of your physical world and to explore the multi-dimensionality of your soul, to remember and rediscover all the knowledge that you have within you as you awaken to your spiritual self?"

"Yes," I said, and I was *inside* the color red at the bottom of the rainbow. I wondered what I'd find inside each color.

Two

Spiritual Search

As I entered the color red inside the rainbow, I felt as if I was wandering through a misty maze — a shimmering space — looking for something special inside me. I wasn't quite sure what I was really looking for, but knew that I'd recognize it immediately when I found it. I knew that I was on a journey in search of my soul, my true spiritual essence.

My search was also about finding my truth, and the meaning and purpose in my life. Somewhere inside my soul, I felt as if I was missing something special in my life, that I had somehow misplaced it, yet knew that I could find it; I could remember it.

Just like the rainbow had offered, I felt as if I was beginning a wonderful adventure that would show me the way to my spiritual knowledge.

I began to look inside my mind, peering into almost-forgotten dreams and misty memories, searching for an image, a clue, a doorway, or a window — a way to remember.

Then I thought of the window in my dream that had opened into the light of a shimmering sunrise.

I began to get clearer on what I was searching for.
I was looking for the answer to something I've
pondered and puzzled over for many years, perhaps
many lifetimes.

I wanted to know who I really am and why I'm
here. I was looking for the realness in my life, for the
meaning and purpose, and what I was meant to do
with my life. But I knew it went much deeper than
that.

I was searching for my spiritual essence, for the
knowledge and truth inside me. I wanted to awaken
my spiritual self, to see through the illusions I'd
enshrouded myself in.

I wanted to see through my physical nature into
the true reality of my spiritual nature. I was looking
for myself — my soul. But where was that to be
found?

I quieted the chatter in my conscious mind and
went within the stillness of myself to meditate,
knowing that the answers I was searching for were
there. But what did the rainbow have to do with all
of this? I wondered.

I sensed that the complete awareness of my true
spiritual nature could be found somewhere inside the
rainbow. Perhaps this was the treasure at the end of
the rainbow that I'd always heard about.

When my search was complete, I could reunite
with myself, encircling the essence of my soul around
me. I knew it would feel as if I was being embraced
with the gentleness and love and joy of my spiritual
self, as if I was coming home. I knew that when I'd

found myself, it would be like giving myself a very special gift.

I don't know how I knew all this; I just *knew* that I knew.

And when I'd found what I've been searching for — my spiritual self — I'd be able to remember all my spiritual knowledge. I also knew that I'd be able to share my knowledge, and to express the pure energy of my soul in every emotion and experience in my life.

I saw a vision of the light of my soul shining and shimmering brightly, like the light of the sunrise.

I was eager to continue the journey on the rainbow path that would guide me into my soul. With this thought, I began to rise into the color orange.

Three

Candle Connection

I seemed to be in a classroom, but I was the only student there. I sat down at a desk and waited for a teacher to appear. I noticed a large, white candle in the center of the room and sensed that this was a meditation class.

Listening to the thoughts inside me, I intuitively knew that I was my own teacher and that no one would appear who could teach me anything that I didn't already know within my soul or that I couldn't learn for myself through my experiences.

It was then that I noticed that the candle had somehow sparkled into a flame — that my thoughts had caused this to occur — and I heard a voice inside my mind. I knew it was my inner voice and I listened to what it said to me.

"It's time for you to know that what you previously thought of as three separate selves — your inner self, your higher self, and your soul — are all one and the same. As you center and focus your awareness, and meditate on the flame of the candle, you'll see how they're intricately interconnected and you'll know how to bring all the levels of your awareness together.

"Your energy essence — your soul — begins within your feelings, and radiates and expands through what you perceive as higher levels of energy. As you center into the energies of your inner self and your feelings, and you raise your awareness, you'll become in tune with the energies of your higher self and your spiritual knowledge.

"As you remember your knowledge, you'll tune into even more aware levels of energy and spiritual vibrations, and you'll become aware of the energies of your soul and your spiritual essence.

"The candle meditation will help you focus and raise your awareness above physical energies by centering your attention on the inner and higher aspects of energy within yourself, above yourself, and into the essence of yourself.

"Focusing on these levels of awareness will put you in touch with the spiritual energies and expressions of your inner self and your higher self, and show you how to tune into the energy vibrations of your soul and your true spiritual self."

I was beginning to understand how these levels of awareness were interwoven and how they all worked together, and was also beginning to feel a sense of oneness with myself, and I hadn't begun to meditate yet. Maybe I knew more than I thought I did, I mused to myself.

My inner voice seemed to acknowledge the knowing inside my mind, then continued as if it — I?

— knew that I wanted more clarity, to better understand myself on all levels.

"The center of the flame represents your inner self and your feelings. The flame of the candle represents your higher self and your spiritual knowledge. The aura, which is the energy essence of the flame, represents your soul.

"Look into the center of the flame of the candle. Focus your attention and awareness into and on the flame of the candle and around the flame at its aura. See and sense it as a complete whole.

"As you focus your thoughts into the center and on the flame, and you sense its energy, you become aware of the energies within you and above you. As you focus your thoughts on the aura around the flame — on the sparkles of light and shimmers of energy that emanate from within and above the flame and expand into the aura surrounding the flame — you become aware of the energies of your soul that encircle your inner self and your higher self.

"By doing this, you see the complete essence of the candle flame — the complete essence of yourself — but you're looking at three separate parts. As you focus individually on the separate parts, you'll become more aware of and in tune with these vibrations of yourself and you'll know how to bring them all together into a unified whole, to see them simultaneously."

It sounded like a wonderful meditation, a way to blend my physical consciousness with my inner feelings, to remember my spiritual knowledge, to become completely aware of my soul, and to bring this awareness into every part of my life. I continued to listen to my inner voice, to the teacher within me.

"Concentrate your awareness into the center of the flame. Feel the energy within you as you enter a more aware level of mind. Feel yourself expanding into an inner level of awareness as you become in tune with the energies of your feelings.

"Look into the center of the flame and feel the energy vibrations of your inner self. Focus into the energies of your feelings as you experience and feel your energy vibrations on a more aware level within you.

"Sense the energy that emanates from within the center of the flame. Become aware of and feel the energy that emanates from within you. Feel the energy that radiates from within the center of your awareness.

"Allow the energies of your inner self and your feelings to expand and flow into a more aware level within yourself. Become more aware of your energy source within, and feel the energy as it begins to expand inside of you. As you become more aware of the energy of your inner self, you become more in touch with your feelings.

"Close your eyes for a few moments to meditate — to focus within on your feelings. Be in touch with your natural awareness of your inner self.

"Become more in tune with the vibrations of your inner self, and more aware of your inner feelings. Go within the center of your awareness, and feel the energy vibrations that form the beginning of your spiritual essence. Become aware of the light and life within you that begins inside your feelings and radiates and expands all around you.

"Feel completely in tune with your inner self, and clearly aware of your energy source within. Become aware of your true feelings that lead you to the truth and knowledge you have within yourself."

I could feel shimmers of warmth beginning to spread within myself, from within the center of my being. I was resonating with the energies of my inner self. I continued to meditate for a while longer, to get even more in tune with my inner self and in touch with my feelings.

"Open your eyes now. Look at the flame of the candle. Focus your attention and your awareness on the entire flame of the candle. Become aware of the energy that emanates from the flame. Begin to raise your energies to a higher level of awareness within yourself. Feel yourself attaining a more aware level of mind.

"As you look at the flame of the candle and you sense its energy, you begin to feel the vibrations of your truth and knowledge opening up inside you and expanding into even higher levels of energy and awareness.

"Focus on the energy within you and begin to feel the energy vibrations of your feelings and your inner truth and knowledge coming together. Begin to feel and sense the energy vibrations of your higher self with your complete consciousness. Become more aware of the energy that emanates from within you and radiates through your inner truth and knowledge.

"Feel the energy that emanates from a higher vibration of truth and knowledge within you. Feel the energy vibration of your higher self and become more aware of the energy that emanates and radiates from your higher self.

"As you become more in tune with your higher levels of energy and awareness, you expand into the awareness of your higher self.

"Feel the increase in the energy vibrations of the knowledge you have within you. Center into your source of knowledge and truth within to reach even higher levels of energy and awareness.

"As you focus on the flame of the candle, you simultaneously focus your feelings and awareness into the higher vibrations of the energy of your truth and knowledge.

"As you feel the vibrations of your higher truth and knowledge opening up and expanding, you become aware of the increased energy that emanates from your higher self and flows from your source of knowledge and truth within.

"As you become aware of your higher source of energy, you become even more aware of your spiritual knowledge — of the truth you have inside your feelings and your mind, and inside your soul. You become more aware of the truth and knowledge you have within yourself; you begin to recognize how they're interwoven with the energies of your inner self and the essence of your soul.

"Close your eyes for a few moments to meditate, to become more aware of and in tune with the energy vibrations of your higher self and to sense how they radiate from within you. See how they flow between your inner self and your soul.

"Become more aware of the truth and knowledge you have within you. Become more and more in tune with the awareness of your higher self, feeling and knowing and remembering the energies that emanate and radiate from your higher self as these energies expand into the awareness of your soul."

I felt as if there was a book opening up inside me, and wondered why that thought had appeared in my mind. Probably because books contain knowledge, I answered myself. At the same time, I felt that knowledge was literally pouring into my mind, reminding me of what I already knew on both an inner and a more aware, higher level within myself.

I could feel myself — my inner awareness and essence — beginning to glow and radiate in rhythm and harmony with the flame of the candle as if I was part of the light — yet knowing at the same time that I *was* the light — again feeling that wonderful, shimmering sense of warmth and resonance spread through my entire body and my mind, encircling my heart and soul at the same time.

I continued to meditate for a while longer, to become more aware of the truth within my feelings and the knowledge within my mind.

"Open your eyes now," my voice — my teacher within — said. The voice was clearer and louder than before. When I'd first heard it and began to listen, it was only a whisper that I could barely hear above the chatter in my mind.

"Look around the flame of the candle at the aura of energy around the flame. The aura is the energy essence of the flame, encircling itself. The aura begins within and radiates from its center, just as the energy and expression of your soul begins within and glows and radiates from the center of your feelings and flows into your knowledge, then expands into your spirituality, forming your energy essence.

"Notice the sparkles around the outside of the flame, how they dance in rhythm and harmony with the flame, with the essence of yourself. Notice how the aura shimmers and moves, how it's alive with energy.

"Focus your awareness around the energy of the flame's aura. Center your awareness into the energy essence of you. Become aware of the energy that emanates from within you, and radiates and expands above you and all around you.

"Begin to feel the energy that emanates from your soul as it goes within itself and then expands outward again. Feel the pure, spiritual vibrations that emanate from within you and radiate through your energy essence.

"Focus your full attention and awareness into your energy essence. See and sense and feel and know and become aware of the energy vibrations of your soul.

"As you become more aware of your energy essence that begins within and expands and radiates all around you, you feel a warm, flowing, fluid movement begin to vibrate inside you — inside your feelings, bringing them together with your spiritual knowledge and blending them with the awareness of your soul."

I had already begun to experience this vibration earlier in the meditation. I smiled to myself; I had always known how to blend my energies together, but had forgotten until now that I innately and intuitively knew how to do this. I also knew that this was a spiritual birthright of every soul.

"As you feel your energy essence glowing within you and radiating all around you, you become more aware of your spiritual energies that transcend physical energies. You become more and more aware that you are a spiritual being.

"Completely encircle yourself with the pure energy vibration of your soul. Feel it radiating from within the center of yourself, opening up and expanding inside you, and forming your aura — your essence.

"Become much more aware of the light and energy that begins within yourself, and emanates and radiates from within the center of your awareness. Become aware of the true essence of your soul; become aware that **you are the energy of light**.

"As you become more and more aware of your soul, the flame becomes brighter and brighter, and the aura around the flame sparkles and shimmers with the increased energy.

"Close your eyes for a few moments to become even more aware of your soul and your energy essence. Become more in tune with the pure energy vibration of your soul. Become more and more aware of your true spiritual nature. See, sense, and feel your energy essence with every part of your awareness.

"Take your time and meditate, being very aware of the energy vibration of your soul."

The shimmering feeling was welling up inside me, even stronger than I'd sensed before in the first two parts of the meditation. It was flowing through me and all around me, resonating with every part of my body, mind, and soul, vibrating warmly in my heart and radiating all around me in sparkles and shimmers of light.

I couldn't find the words to describe it, though it felt familiar and I knew I'd experienced it before in some of the spiritual experiences in my life when I'd truly been in touch with my soul. And there were other times that I'd felt and experienced this feeling in another part of my awareness, *somewhere* inside a special, sacred place in my soul.

I continued to meditate, feeling the essence of my soul vibrating in perfect harmony and synchronicity with my inner feelings and my spiritual knowledge.

"Open your eyes now and look at the candle flame. Look into the center of the flame and completely tune into your inner feelings. Look above the flame and completely tune into your higher truth and knowledge. Look around the flame and completely tune into the essence of your soul.

"Bring all these levels of awareness together within yourself. Bring the energy of your feelings, the awareness of your truth and knowledge, and the energy essence of your soul together into a unity of understanding.

"Consciously absorb everything you've become aware of in this candle meditation. Bring the complete awareness and understanding of your inner self, your higher self, and your soul — your energy essence — into every part of your body, heart, mind, and soul."

I felt a powerful energy and awareness spreading and flowing within me, from within the center of my being, rising up above me and vibrating in harmony all around me, knowing that what I had just experienced within the energies of my inner self, my higher self, and my soul had brought me into a oneness and harmony with myself.

I no longer felt separate from myself. I was a completely spiritual being, whole within myself. I felt as if I'd found the missing pieces of myself and brought them together.

My inner voice — my teacher within, my soul — said to me, "The candle meditation helps you to become more aware of the energies of your inner self, your higher self, and the essence of your soul. It helps you attain a more spiritual level of mind by focusing your awareness into the energies of yourself."

I knew how special and spiritual this meditation was, and I also knew that in every moment of my life, I could instantly attain this level of mind again — this complete spiritual awareness and togetherness with myself — at any time, no matter where I was or what I was doing.

And every time I did this — on a conscious, more aware level — I would become even more aware of and in tune with my inner self, my higher self, and my soul, and I'd be able to bring them closer and connect them more together in harmony. I knew that this was a very special gift from the rainbow, given to myself.

I was resonating with the rainbow and remembered my feelings when I'd first entered the rainbow in my dream, when I felt the rainbow all around me and within me and I'd become a rainbow of colors, expanding both inward and outward.

It seemed that my dream was much more than a dream; it was becoming more and more real, and I felt as if I was becoming more awake and aware.

I had a sense — a real feeling of knowing — that my inner teacher was more than she appeared to be. She was more than a rainbow; she was a way-shower, a light-being from the Universe, shining her light and radiance upon the Earth.

Maybe I'm a spiritual sun ray, I thought to myself, smiling as I imagined myself shining and shimmering my light upon the Earth.

My voice continued speaking and this time I really heard it inside my soul. "By doing this meditation, you raised your level of awareness and your spiritual energy vibrations. You increased and brought together your understanding of your inner feelings with your truth and knowledge, blending them with all the experiences in your life."

And with all the experiences in my dreams, I added silently to myself.

"At the same time, you began to see through the illusions of your physical reality into the true awareness of your soul. You also began opening up and remembering your spiritual knowledge."

Where do we go from here? I wondered, beginning to feel like a free spirit.

My voice answered, "You can expand your awareness even further, into the multi-dimensionality of your soul."

Like a butterfly that emerges from its cocoon and spreads its wings to fly — to soar into the sky, the Universe and beyond, I mused.

"As you become more aware of and in tune with the energy vibrations of your inner self, your higher self, and your soul, you become aware of the true nature of all your experiences.

"As you blend and bring together the energies of your feelings, knowledge, and the awareness of the essence of your soul into the complete wisdom and unity of understanding, you become aware of the true nature of your spirituality."

Suddenly I heard the most beautiful music and wondered where it was coming from. It sounded like a celestial chorus singing inside my body, my heart, my mind, and my soul.

The words echoed in my mind, repeating themselves through the simultaneous vibrations of my inner self, my higher self, and my soul — blending perfectly into my spiritual self — the essence of me.

"As you understand and tune into the energies that are the essence of you, and you unify the energies into a harmony of understanding, you feel and know and are aware of your soul and the true nature of your spirituality — the true essence of yourself."

I'd always sensed within me that my feelings, my knowledge, and my soul were one and the same, but could never seem to bring them all together until now. It was so wonderful to be a whole person, not scattered or separate from myself.

This dream — if it was a dream; it was beginning to feel very real — was getting better all the time. I felt as if I was waking up inside the dream, inside my awareness. I was beginning to recognize, and to really know, that the rainbow voice was my own voice.

I wanted more knowledge. I wanted to know more about myself, about my soul. With this thought, I began to rise into the color yellow inside the rainbow. I remembered reading somewhere that the color yellow was the color of knowledge.

Four

Light Library

Maybe I could go to the library and find a book that would give me more knowledge. The image of that thought showed me a spiral stairway shimmering with light.

Placing my foot on the bottom step, I felt a gentle wave of energy flow through me. Traveling up the stairs, the vibration of energy softly radiated upward from my feet through my entire body.

I began to feel as if I was floating a few inches above the steps, gliding through emanations of energy, weightless and free, flowing into higher realms of light.

The top of the stairs were shrouded in a soft, white mist. As I entered the mist, it cleared, showing a vibrant path shimmering with light.

Following the path, I felt the pure white light vibrating gently all around me, filling me with a wonderful feeling of peace and harmony.

A few steps ahead, I saw a building that was illuminated with the shimmering white light. The building emanated and radiated a special kind of energy.

The light welcomed me within. Entering the library, I noticed that it was created entirely with the vibrant energy of the light itself. Light was every-where. Rays of universal light flowed in through the open windows. Vibrations of light formed the floors and the walls. Beams of sparkling energy supported the arched ceiling; in the center was a domed skylight.

A magical aura surrounded the library; ethereal energies of pure awareness softly reverberated through the vast array of books. A hushed stillness echoed within the library even as it shimmered with energy, with the knowledge contained in the books that filled the shelves and lined the walls.

As I listened quietly, I heard the books talk in whispers of wisdom and murmurs of mystical knowl-edge.

The rows of books appeared to be endless, as if they went on forever. Walking through the aisles and the alcoves, I saw books on every subject imaginable and knew that this library contained all the knowl-edge that had ever been written or recorded, in all the world and the entire Universe, since the beginning of time, since the beginning of thought.

Running my fingers over the titles of the books, I discovered that I could read them within my mind. The books were written in a universal language that I understood easily, just by touching the books or looking at the pictures on the covers.

The words and their images danced into my mind, creating a symphony of sound vibrations, and within the music and the melody, I understood the knowledge inside each book.

Continuing to walk through the library, exploring the light energies of knowledge, I noticed another stairway with seven steps that vibrated with a light more dazzling, more brilliant than the light that surrounded the open entrance to the library.

The light shimmered and sparkled with energy, as if it was alive. I sensed a sacred feeling about this light; it seemed to contain an essence within itself.

The vibrations emanating from this light were filled with images of color that had shape and substance. It looked like a beautiful blur of rainbow colors in a gentle wave of motion, forming into ever-changing transparent prisms of light.

Looking into the light, I experienced an emotion that went beyond words and thoughts, and I knew that I was about to enter a very sacred space inside my soul.

More than anything else, I wanted to be part of that light. I wanted to rush into the light, to become the essence of the light, yet felt that I might disturb it if I rushed, so I waited, respectfully and reverently.

The light opened up and invited me in, just as the light at the entrance to the library had welcomed me within. Stepping into the light, I was filled with a feeling of awe and wonderment and pure joy.

Each step of the stairway vibrated in harmony with the colors of a rainbow. Walking slowly, thoughtfully, up the stairs, I paused on every step — feeling the energy, hearing the unique vibration, the tone and hue and experience of each color.

Ascending the stairs and absorbing the colors within my body, my mind, and my feelings — within every part of me in perfect harmony, I became more and more aware of my soul.

As my awareness expanded, I knew that I was traveling a stairway that would lead me into the true essence of myself. As I experienced my awareness flowing into and through the vibrations of the rainbow, I felt as if I was flying through the energies of muted sounds and colors.

Reaching the top of the stairs, I saw that the higher echelon of the library was a loft that contained the written records of every soul's existence and I knew, with an absolute knowing, that these books vibrated with a light that was unique to every soul and that they could only be opened and read by that particular soul.

In the center of the loft, I saw a table with an open book and a lamp that glowed with a luminous light. Next to the table was a comfortable chair. I walked over to the table and looked at the book. It seemed that the library had been waiting for me to discover it, and the open book had been waiting to be read by me.

Knowing that this book was about my soul, I looked at the chapter title that the book was opened to — *Follow Your Dream: A Rainbow Path Into Awakening*.

As I read the words, they began to vibrate on the page, then to shimmer with a soft glow of lavender light, radiating into rays of energy that formed images that swirled into my thoughts and sparkled into pictures, opening a special kind of knowing within my mind. Touching the words, my hand began to vibrate with energy.

I realized how very special this book was. Picking it up, I settled comfortably in the chair. Holding the open book in my hands, my body began to vibrate with a radiant energy. I felt as if I was being drawn inside the pages of the book as the words vibrated and resonated in my mind, moving in rhythm and harmony with the flow of spiritual and universal energy.

It felt as if a gentle current of energy was flowing through me, opening up and releasing a higher awareness within. I heard a soft humming sound inside my mind, and as the energy continued to softly flow through me, I knew that my spiritual awareness was opening up inside me, beginning to surge and soar through every part of my body, mind, and soul.

This is so wonderful, so magical, I thought, smiling to myself, a special smile that I understood deep inside my soul. Hugging the book close to my heart, I knew I'd found a very special treasure — a book that reveals all my spiritual knowledge, a book that shows me the secrets of my soul.

As I read the chapter title again, the words formed an image that drew complete and detailed pictures in my mind. I touched the pictures in the book — the pictures in my mind — feeling the texture of the images. The pictures were solid. The scene was real; it wasn't an image that disappeared when I blinked my eyes.

The words formed real pictures. When I read the words, they formed pictures that came to life — three-dimensional images that vibrated from the pages into my awareness, into my physical reality — resonating with an energy source that was inspired by the words on the pages.

The book was energy in motion and the words magically transported me inside my rainbow dream. I was there, inside the picture; I was really there. Looking around myself, I saw and felt and experienced everything there was to see and feel and experience.

I saw the candle. I saw a magical forest with a tree that talked to me, and a shimmering white cloud in an azure-blue sky that transported me everywhere I wanted to go. I saw a music box that played beautiful music inside my soul when I opened it. I watched the birth of a butterfly as it emerged from its chrysalis and I became the butterfly as it flew somewhere over the rainbow and soared into the Universe.

And then I was sitting on a beach watching the dawn of a new day, enjoying the light of the sun and I traveled a magical sun ray beyond the spectrum of the sunrise into the light of my soul.

The book was filled with every experience I'd ever had or will have, and yet I knew I could write and rewrite the pages and paragraphs in any way that I chose.

As I looked through the pages and read the words that had already been written, my experiences came to life and I completely understood — with a clarity and knowing that went beyond words — why they had happened and why I had chosen to experience them.

I felt — with every part of myself, with every part of my awareness — the events and emotions inside my experiences as the words drew detailed and descriptive images and scenes within my mind.

The book was timeless as it portrayed the pictures of my soul — the essence of my spirit — in my mind, as it spoke to me of the events and emotions in my life, and showed me all the many, various aspects of all my experiences in every time frame — past, present, and future, and in every dimension of being, in every realm of my awareness.

The book showed me the true reality of me, the true multi-dimensionality of my soul. This is the best book I've ever read, I thought to myself. Or written, I added silently, remembering that in my real life, I'm a writer.

Or is this dream my real life? It seemed that they were both one and the same. It also seemed that every part of my dream was opening me up to an increased level of awareness and understanding of my spiritual self as I traveled higher and higher into and through the colors of the rainbow.

I was beginning to feel a bit overwhelmed with all the experiences I was having and the awareness that was opening up inside of me, and with wanting to completely open up all the spiritual knowledge that I knew I had within me.

I decided to go for a walk through nature to ponder my thoughts and to absorb my experiences within me when I heard my rainbow voice in my mind.

"You've come a long way from when you first entered the rainbow in your dream to follow your path to awakening your spiritual self. Are you ready to continue on the rainbow path that leads you within to truly become a free spirit and to find your own special place in the sun where you can be the spiritual person that you really are and always were?"

I nodded yes, beginning to flow into the color green, knowing that my physical self was really a mirror of my spiritual self and that I was ready to more fully awaken within myself.

Five

Magical Forest

Arriving in the color green, I saw a magical forest surrounded with a softly-swirling white mist, or perhaps it was sunbeams — rays of light — and they only appeared to be misty because of the clouds floating above and through the forest.

Maybe I was ready to see through the mist, into the clear light of my soul, I thought to myself.

The scene was enchanting, like something out of a movie and yet I knew that it was very real. I sensed that it was a special, sacred place where I knew inside me that I could become even more aware of my true essence — my real self — and that I could rediscover and reclaim all the joys and treasures and gifts that my spiritual self has to offer me.

It was a warm, pleasant summer day, the most beautiful one that I've ever experienced. I remembered the dream I'd just had — or was I still dreaming? — when I rose through the colors inside the rainbow and began to rediscover the magical, mystical secrets of my soul, and now I was ready to travel further along the path that led me within. I knew that the rainbow was there in the sunshine, somewhere.

The forest beckoned me, inviting me to experience the peace I felt within myself and to feel connected with the Earth, to appreciate the beauty of nature and to experience the harmony of the Earth with the Universe, the harmony of my physical self with my spiritual self.

I wanted to experience again the wonder and awe of the natural world all around me as I began to fully open up and explore the spiritual world within me. Deep inside myself, I knew that I was part of that special connection between the Earth and the Universe and I wanted to feel that again.

The day was filled with the quiet sounds of nature; I could feel and hear the gentle breeze as it touched me and moved softly through the leaves of the trees in the forest ahead of me.

Walking toward the trees, I felt the warmth and energy of the sun and I began to experience the sense of aliveness and vibrancy that being in nature brings me.

Breathing in deeply, I felt the pure, clean air circulate through my lungs, revitalizing and rejuvenating every part of me. As this physical/universal energy flowed through my body and my mind, touching my heart and my spirit, I felt lighter and happier.

Breathing out, I let go of all my cares and worries. I could feel them slip away as I enjoyed this beautiful day, this wonderful walk through nature.

Following the path that led me within, I entered the forest. The sunshine sparkled and shimmered through the tops of the trees, creating patterns and playing with shafts of light on the forest floor.

I noticed how intricate the patterns were, and how they were constantly moving and changing. I compared them to my experiences, and how my experiences were constantly changing in harmony with my thoughts and feelings, moving in rhythm with my mind's awareness.

Walking through the open, airy forest, I felt as if I was walking on a soft bed of Earth. I noticed how quiet it was inside the forest, and how peaceful it was. I began to enter a meditative frame of mind — a special, serene place within myself where I felt completely comfortable and natural.

I saw a circular clearing up ahead and the sunlight beckoned me forth, welcoming me. I knew that I'd been here before, inside this sacred space within myself — this sacred space inside my thoughts and dreams.

I felt perfectly at home and centered within myself, in tune with nature, as I walked slowly into the clearing, completely enjoying the feelings of peace and harmony within myself and all around me.

I gazed up at the sun shining brightly in the sky. The mists that I'd seen earlier had dissipated and disappeared.

I heard a tree calling to me and walked to the side of the clearing. Gently touching the tree, and hugging it as if it were an old and very dear friend, I sat quietly on the soft ground for a few minutes next to it.

Then leaning back against the tree, I closed my eyes, listening to my thoughts and watching their images move in my mind.

The gentle breeze created a light, musical sound that vibrated in harmony within my mind as the wind blew softly through the leaves of the tree. The leaves whispered in the wind and through my mind, sharing the secrets of nature with me.

Somehow I knew that I could communicate with the tree, and I listened as it told me about its connection with the Earth and the Universe, about how its roots are connected to the Earth as its branches reach outward and upward to touch the sky, and even higher, to embrace the Universe.

The tree spoke to me of the harmony that is within nature, the harmony that the Earth and the Universe shares with nature, the harmony that I share between my physical self and my spiritual self, the harmony that exists between my inner and outer worlds.

The tree told me that the Universe is within me and that I am the Universe, expressing myself — my spiritual nature — in physical form.

After a while, I opened my eyes. Looking up at the sky, I saw a few shimmering, white clouds floating leisurely by, and I noticed how blue and expansive the sky was. It seemed to go on forever, beyond the horizon into the Universe and even farther than that into infinity. I wondered what it would be like to float on one of those puffy white clouds.

The sky had an ethereal quality — a magical,

mystical essence that I couldn't describe with words — a majesty that I've known before but haven't experienced for a long time. Breathing in deeply, I absorbed every part of the blueness within myself; the color filled me with a wonderful sense of inner peace and awareness, a sense of knowing within my mind.

As I breathed in the blueness of the sky, I felt a more aware level of communication opening up inside me between my inner self and my spiritual self, between my conscious and subconscious mind. I knew that I could really listen to and hear myself on all levels of my awareness, and that I could also tune into nature and commune with all of nature. I felt at one with nature and at one within myself.

Standing up, I felt as if I could reach up through the sky and touch the Universe. Stretching my arms upward in an open embrace toward the sky, I felt a magical surge of energy and awareness inside me, knowing that I am part of the Earth and the Universe, in harmony with the physical world around me and the spiritual world within me.

I sensed how infinite these worlds really are and I began to rediscover how infinite I really am. I began to recognize that I am a powerful, spiritual being. I began to remember the full awareness that I have within me, within my mind and my soul. I began to feel my true spiritual nature opening up inside me, expanding into the Universe.

I decided to continue walking, to explore every-thing I saw, to totally experience and understand both the world around me and the world within me. I moved in rhythm and harmony with my mind's awareness that was opening up more completely.

Reaching the edge of the forest, I entered a field of flowers growing wild and free in a meadow. Walking through them, I sensed how truly alive the flowers are; I sensed how special and magical they are.

Breathing in their wonderful fragrance, I sensed their inner essence and I became aware of how they're connected to both the Earth and the Universe, just as I am. I became aware of their natural harmony with the world around them and the world within them, just as I sensed and experienced the natural harmony of my physical self with my spiritual self.

The flowers were vibrantly alive, flowing with the natural energy of life and their spiritual essence, and I knew that I was even more vibrantly alive, flowing with the essence of my spirituality. This knowing — this feeling — welled up inside me, growing and expanding.

I began to run, to express my awareness opening up inside me and to feel my own spiritual energy vibrating inside my physical body. Running joyfully through the meadow, totally experiencing and enjoying my freedom and energy, I felt the wind in my hair and the gentle warmth of the sun on my face. I felt as if I was a child again, free and completely happy.

Ahead of me, the meadow turned into a gently sloping valley. As I slowed down and looked into the valley, I saw how green and healthy and vibrant and beautiful everything was. The sun radiated sparkles of light from a softly-winding stream of water in the center and I heard the sound of a waterfall.

Stopping to listen to the sound, I knew, as if I'd been here before, that the waterfall was hidden just beyond the bushes and boulders that I saw on my right.

Walking that way, I could smell the water and almost see a rainbow. Smiling to myself, I knew that the rainbow I saw in my mind was real and that I'd found the path that leads me within to my true spiritual self.

Parting the bushes, I saw a magnificent waterfall gushing with life as it cascaded into a gentle, quiet pool beneath. Every drop of water caught the sunlight and reflected a beautiful, shimmering rainbow.

I followed the footpath down through the lush, flowering bushes to where the waterfall entered the clear, sparkling pool.

Kneeling down to run my fingers through the water, I looked into the pool and saw more than the reflection of my physical self. Shimmering in the water was the essence of my inner, spiritual self, moving around and through my image in gentle ripples.

I noticed how the water mirrored and reflected the sky above me and I recognized that my physical self is really a mirror of my spiritual self, and that all my experiences in every dimension of reality and awareness reflect the knowledge I have within me.

At the same time, I remembered and realized the infinite reality of my soul and that my soul mirrors both the Earth and the Universe.

And I knew that the reality of my physical experiences goes much deeper than my conscious mind, much farther than the physical world. Below the surface, and all around me in every experience, thought, and feeling, my inner awareness — my spiritual self waits — ever so quietly to be recognized, to be heard.

As I began to more fully open up both my physical consciousness and my spiritual awareness, I heard my inner voice whispering to me in my thoughts and feelings, and through my dreams and experiences.

As I listened, I knew that I could feel and become completely aware of all the vibrations of all my experiences as I traveled through them, following my rainbow path that leads me within to my spiritual self.

Six

Clearing Clouds

Am I awake or am I dreaming? I wondered, rising up into the color blue inside the rainbow.

I was outside on a beautiful, sunny day, laying in a softly-swaying hammock, just enjoying the gentle breeze and the warmth and light of the sunshine.

Looking up at the sky, I saw a few shimmering white clouds floating leisurely by and I noticed how blue and expansive the sky was, just like it had been in the clearing in the forest when I'd wondered what it would be like to float on one of those puffy white clouds.

Blue, I remembered somewhere in my mind, was the color of communication. Maybe I could talk to the cloud, to see what it has to say. Or maybe I could communicate with the sky, to open a universal channel of awareness and clarity.

I again wondered, this time with more intent, what it would be like to float leisurely through the sky on a light, fluffy cloud. Would it be the same as swinging gently in my hammock or would it be completely different? Would it change my perceptions or my perspective of things? Would it help to clear some cloudiness in my mind, and to open up a universal understanding?

The thoughts gently projected my awareness into the blueness of the sky. I was up on that fluffy white cloud, floating along, feeling free and light, weightless, unrestrained by gravity and physical restrictions.

It was a wonderful feeling to be so free and light. The cloud supported me with a cushiony softness that was unlike anything else I've ever experienced. It was as if I was made up of the essence of the cloud itself, yet I knew that my essence — my awareness — was distinctly different.

As the cloud floated along, directed by unseen universal winds, I began to wonder where it was going but this thought didn't really concern me. I was quite content to just go with the flow, to be completely here now in the present moment, to experience the calm, relaxing feeling of simply floating on the gentle breeze.

Every once in a while, I peered over the side of the cloud and looked down at the Earth, knowing I could return at any time simply by thinking the thought.

Even though the cloud seemed to be drifting in the wind, I knew that there was a universal direction that it follows, a natural flow of energy, a divine plan, and that this cloud has its own purpose for being, its special mission in life.

I wondered what that purpose might be, so I

merged my consciousness with the cloud's consciousness to discover its reason for existence. Surprisingly,
the cloud had a lot to say. Inside its misty, ethereal
appearance as a wispy white cloud, it had a definite
purpose for being, and contained within itself was its
universal essence. Seemingly floating aimlessly along,
it has seen and experienced many wonderful and
magical things.

It has traveled the world in many forms:
Sometimes as the puffy white cloud it is now floating
softly on a gentle breeze. Sometimes seeming to dis-
appear and dissipate in the light of the sun, changing
its shape and substance, reappearing when it draws
moisture from the Earth, being nourished from its
physical source, and in turn, nurturing the Earth with
universal energy.

Sometimes it appears as a powerful cloud, rolling
and roaring through the sky as it thunders and
creates bold streaks of lightning, invigorating and
energizing the Earth. Sometimes pouring rain, and
other times providing a gentle shower of rain, sharing
universal nourishment with the Earth.

It was always there, in one form or another,
fulfilling its divine purpose, just like I'm always here,
in one form or another, following my path and
fulfilling my divine purpose.

I became aware that even though at times, it
seems that my life appears to be like this luminous
cloud as it was expressing itself at this particular
moment — seemingly drifting aimlessly along,
floating through the sky — that there is a unique and
very special purpose that I have in life, just as every

soul has.

I was floating along for the moment, letting my thoughts meander through my mind while gathering information and energy that will manifest in one form or another for a particular purpose.

For now, I was going with the flow, free and easy, soft and serene, feeling a bit philosophical, lightly pondering the possibilities and probabilities of future actions and experiences I was planning in my physical reality, and at the same time, playing with metaphors and listening to the muse in my mind.

Maybe I'll write a book about this rainbow dream, I thought dreamily to myself.

Perfectly content to travel softly and easily on this puffy white cloud, I continued to float along, thinking my thoughts and knowing that everything I do and experience is part of a perfect plan that I've created for myself, and that all the events in my life have a special purpose, meaning, and reason for existence.

I knew that there were many other things this cloud could tell me and share with me, and that there were many special, magical things that it could show and offer me.

But for now, I just wanted to float through the sky, above the Earth, above the physical reality of my existence, being in the blueness, thinking my thoughts and knowing that this cloud was my magic carpet ride to anywhere I wanted to go and that it was also a mentor for my thoughts.

Just like the cloud, I was going with the flow,

being in the present moment, enjoying the journey of simply being here now, experiencing how wonderful and free this cloud is, and how wonderful and free I am within my thoughts and feelings, and within my spirituality.

Suddenly I was back in my hammock, swaying softly in the gentle breeze, looking up at the shimmering white clouds in the sky, clearly knowing the mysteries of my mind and the magic of my true spiritual nature, and understanding how infinite and multi-dimensional my awareness is.

I smiled up at the cloud and to myself, knowing that I've rediscovered some wonderful and magical things. I've rediscovered that my consciousness exists both within and separately from my physical body, and that my thoughts are free to travel on the energy of air inside what appears to be a white, misty cloud of illusion in the sky.

I've learned how to see through my physical reality from a higher, spiritual perspective. And I've remembered how to fly.

Seven

Mystical Music Box

Continuing to follow my dream into the color indigo — a deep purplish-blue, I entered a quiet, warmly-lit room and I sensed — I knew — that there was a wonderful treasure here, a special, spiritual gift that drew me into this subdued, sacred place inside my soul.

Looking around, I noticed a small, delicately decorated music box. Opening it, I heard a beautiful melody begin to play. The sounds were harmonious and gentle, soft and soothing, inviting me into a peaceful place within myself.

Delighted, I closed my eyes to more fully experience and appreciate the music as it richly filled every part of the acoustically-perfect room — as it deeply filled all my senses and every part of my awareness with pure enjoyment — as it shimmered softly into and through my body, heart, mind, and soul.

I listened to the music inside myself as it lightly resonated through my body, into my feelings and the thoughts inside my mind, played gently through my heart, and softly sang into my soul.

I completely tuned into the harmony of the tones and sounds of the feelings that the music inspired and brought forth within me. I felt myself — my awareness — expanding, ever-so-gently, into the rhythm and tune and melody of my spiritual essence.

As my awareness expanded into the music, it became part of me, and I became part of the music. I knew that the music I heard came from a place of memory deep within me, from the knowingness of my soul.

The music box played the celestial song of the Universe — the symphony of my soul. The song sang to me of home, calling to me softly and gently. This magical, mystical music box played a melody of harmony, peace, joy, and love within me — the natural, spiritual vibration of my soul, inspiring and opening up remembrances inside of me.

Listening to the melody, I remembered that once upon a time I was a rainbow, then I came back down to Earth as a free spirit in physical form and I magically metamorphosed into a butterfly inside my mind; it was a spiritually symbolic way of remembering my true spiritual nature and seeing through physical illusions.

Then I became a writer and went to the library to read an interesting, informative, and enlightening book about my soul. The book reminded me that I was part of the sunrise and as I began to awaken from a wonderful dream, with traces of this magical melody — this celestial music — playing in my mind, I understood the symphony of the stars as they shared the secrets of the Universe and the song of my soul.

The music transported me into a shimmering sphere of lavender light inside a magical, mystical dream — a dream within a dream — as I began to enter the color violet at the top of the rainbow.

I was in a multi-dimensional place within my soul, a transparent, luminous space within the Universe, within my mind, where every thought, feeling, and experience is real, and they all happen simultaneously in my here and now, in the present moment.

What a concept, I thought to myself. And it all started with a song that shimmered into my awareness, with one verse — the Universe.

Eight

Free Spirit

If all my thoughts are real, and they happen — they become experiences — before, during, and after I think them, then I'm creating millions of experiences at the same time, and how can I be aware of them all?

It was mind-boggling, like trying to catch butter-flies on a windy day as they flitted through various stages of my awareness.

Pondering the many myriad aspects of my thoughts, I found myself in a mystical field of flowers, similar to the meadow beyond the forest, but this meadow vibrated with a special, sacred energy.

The meadow was multi-dimensional, forming and reforming itself in every moment. It glowed with a shimmering violet light and everything seemed ethereal and transparent, even though it looked solid at the same time.

I realized that nothing was really as it appeared to be. Listening to my thoughts, I knew that my true nature was that of a free spirit, dressed in a physical body.

I *knew* — with every part of my knowing — that I am a spiritual being and that I am more than my physical self, much more than my physical body and my mind.

I *knew* that my soul wasn't limited in any way by physical energies, and that I could expand my awareness and transcend the limits and restrictions of what appeared to be my physical reality.

I *knew* that my soul vibrated to spiritual and universal energies, in tune with nature and the Universe, moving in rhythm with knowledge and awareness, in harmony with light. My soul was the universal energy of light, and I knew that I could feel and experience my spirit in its pure energy form.

Listening to my thoughts, I compared my soul to a butterfly that's free, moving on wings of spiritual and universal energies. I knew that I could unwrap the physical cocoon of earthly energies and break through the paper-like shell of limited consciousness to fully open up my awareness and set my spirit free.

A movement in a nearby bush caught my attention. I saw a beautiful, rainbow-colored butterfly emerging from its golden chrysalis. Watching its birth, I realized that I was seeing something very special and magical.

The butterfly had just emerged into the light and was beginning to open its wings to fly, to explore its new life as a transformed being — as a free spirit. As the butterfly expanded its wings, they shimmered in the sunlight and I realized that, in essence, I am very much like the butterfly.

I felt at one with it and in harmony with the world around me and within me. I began to understand what the butterfly feels like as it frees itself and begins to fly, floating on natural currents of air, enjoying the light of the sunshine all around it, rising and soaring into the sky and through the clouds into the Universe.

I felt as if I could rise and soar with the butterfly, in harmony with air and light. I felt as if I could rise and soar into the Universe, transcending the illusions of physical boundaries and limits, moving upward through the clouds into the light of my spiritual energies. I felt as if I could rise even higher into universal energies, where my soul is open and free in its true form.

Becoming more in tune with the energies of the butterfly — with the energies of my spiritual nature — I felt as if I was the butterfly and I understood its natural harmony with the Universe. Simultaneously I became aware of my natural harmony with the Universe; I became aware that I could transcend earthly energies and flow into universal energies of awareness and light.

Bringing this awareness into my mind, I began to feel myself opening up and expanding through the energies of my physical reality, transforming myself into the vibration of my spiritual self.

Blending into my spiritual awareness, I began to feel even more open and expansive and free, much like how I imagine the butterfly felt when it peered through and released itself from its transparent, paper-like cocoon.

As I watched the butterfly fully open up and expand its wings and begin to fly, expressing itself as a free spirit, I began to fully open up and expand my spiritual awareness.

Flowing and floating upward into higher vibrations of awareness and light, I became in tune with my spiritual energies and I felt the essence of my soul.

As I experienced this, I felt myself — my awareness — blending into the energies of the Universe, in harmony with my true spiritual nature.

As the butterfly continued to float and fly, I felt myself floating and flying even higher, emerging and expanding into knowledge and light. The butterfly was free — flying, soaring above the Earth — and I was just as free.

I was free of the clouds of physical energies, free of the illusions; I'd emerged into the energy of my soul. I felt my spirit begin to fly and soar and expand into ever-higher realms and realities of knowledge and awareness and light.

Flying and soaring upward, higher and higher, I felt the freedom of knowledge and the light of awareness. Floating on natural currents of air and energy, I felt my spirit becoming more and more free.

As I continued to rise into the true awareness of my spirit, I saw sparkles and shimmers of light — rays of sunshine and the radiance of stars — that illuminated both the sky and the Universe. They were vibrant with energy and felt nourishing and nurturing as they showered me with awareness, as they showered the Earth with light.

Absorbing the light and energy, I felt very vibrant and nourished from the Universe and nurtured from within myself, knowing that I was really a free spirit and that I was experiencing the energies of the true nature of my soul.

I felt illuminated with the energy of the Universe — in tune with my spiritual essence, with the light of sunshine and the vibrant radiance of the stars — with the energy of my inner truth and knowledge, and the light of my spiritual awareness.

I continued to fly and soar upward, higher and higher, becoming more and more free — transcending the earthly pull of physical energies, expanding into ever-widening horizons of true knowledge and awareness — flying on shimmering wings of illumination and light.

My spirit was free, flying and soaring and expanding into the Universe, moving with the motion and rhythm of knowledge and awareness and light.

I was somewhere over the rainbow.

Nine

Beyond the Spectrum of the Sunrise

As I began to wake up, I remembered my rainbow dream. Looking through the open window, I noticed that it was nearly dawn and wondered what it would be like to be a sunrise. I decided to find out.

I'd read somewhere in a book that sunrises hold a promise of a wonderful discovery — the dawn of a new beginning, the dawn of a new light beginning within you, and that if you could travel beyond the spectrum of the sunrise, into the center of the sun, you'd find a magical treasure inside your soul.

I felt a gentle, warm breeze coming in through the window and could smell the fresh scent of the morning air and the wonderful aroma of the wet Earth that was recently nourished from the rain.

I arose and went outside to see the sunrise. Looking up at the sky, I saw the rainbow shimmering in the pre-dawn light, offering to be my guide — my way-shower — into the light of my soul.

"Perhaps you're ready to explore and experience

the light within yourself as you travel beyond the spectrum of the sunrise," the rainbow said to me. "Perhaps you're ready to completely remember your spiritual knowledge and to rediscover the mystical awareness of your soul."

I wondered if that was the treasure.

Listening to my thoughts and watching their images move in my mind, I remembered when I walked through the forest and reconnected with myself — with my true spiritual nature — and I rediscovered the harmony of the Earth with the Universe, the harmony between my physical self and my spiritual self. I remembered the tree that told me the secrets of nature — the secrets of my soul — telling me that the Universe was within myself.

I remembered the wonderful waterfall that created shimmering rainbows everywhere, and when I looked into the quiet pool beneath, I saw both my physical self and my spiritual self mirrored together in the water and I became aware of how the Earth is a mirror of the Universe, just as I am a physical mirror of my spiritual self.

I remembered another time when I felt in harmony with myself and in tune with my true nature. I remembered how I'd communed with the natural essence of myself. It seemed to be a long time ago, as if it had happened somewhere in a dream within a dream.

As I listened to my thoughts, I knew that there was a beach nearby because I could hear the sound of the waves. I thought I'd enjoy the sunrise even more if I was there.

Arriving at the beach, I saw a perfect place to watch the sunrise. Sitting on the sand and looking at the waves as they gently touched the shore, I felt a wonderful sense of peace and harmony within myself and all around me.

I felt as if I was returning to my true spiritual nature. Listening to the rhythmic ebb and flow of the tide, I felt at one with myself and in harmony with the Earth and the Universe.

Looking across the water and up at the sky, I had a clear view of the horizon as the water seemingly touched the sky. I saw a few misty clouds above the horizon and noticed that they were tinged with the early colors of dawn.

Mauve, then pale orange blending into a beautiful mixture of coral and pink that combined into fuchsia colored the bottom of the clouds and splashed across the sky.

The beauty and misty softness of the colors inspired a sense of awe and wonderment inside me as I realized that I was seeing more than the colors of dawn, the colors of a new day; I was seeing the colors of a new beginning.

I noticed that the sky was getting lighter. As the light from the sun began to shine behind and through the clouds, dissipating the mistiness, I saw the first rays of the sunrise come over the horizon and noticed how the light was mirrored and reflected on the water.

The light of this sunrise was tinged and colored with a wonderful feeling of energy and awareness and clarity. It radiated a vibrant energy as it emanated rays of light in tones and hues that resonated with the rhythm of my soul. I sensed that this sunrise was very special. It was more than magical; it was mystical.

I felt the light of the sun softly surrounding me as it gently entered my body, mind, and soul, filling me with universal energy and spiritual awareness.

I was vibrating in harmony with the light of the sun, with the radiant energy. Feeling and sensing the sunrise with every part of me, I was drawn into the light of the sunrise, knowing that I was ready to remember all my knowledge and fully awaken my spiritual self.

Somewhere within me — within my mind and soul — I realized that I was the colors of dawn, and I began to recognize the light dawning within me.

Just as the water had reflected the beginning of the sunrise, I knew that the sunrise in the sky — mirrored within my mind — was a reflection of my spiritual awareness — my inner knowing — opening up within me, awakening me to the knowledge within myself.

The sunlight sparkled and shimmered on the water, reflecting the light of the Universe. Centering my awareness into the light of the sunrise, it became brighter and brighter, illuminating every part of me, filling me with pure enlightenment. I knew that the sunrise was within me and that I was the sunrise.

The sun was above the horizon now and as the sun continued to rise in the sky, I rose with it —

higher and higher. The feeling was exhilarating and I felt more alive and awake and aware than I've ever felt before.

I remembered that there was a special place that I knew of, a magical place that was beyond the colors of dawn, beyond the spectrum of the sunrise. Going into and through and beyond the light of the sunrise, I entered that special and most magical place within myself.

It felt as if I was coming home, as if I was returning to myself. I knew that I'd been here before in this sacred place inside my soul, where I'd communed with the natural essence of myself, and that I've always known the way to this most special, magical, mystical place.

From within this place, I saw that the sun was beginning to rise in the center of myself, in the center of my awareness, in the center of my soul. As I became more aware of my spiritual essence, a pure white light — a light brighter than the sunrise — entered into every part of my awareness.

I could feel the light vibrating all around me and within me. I could feel this light — this energy of spiritual awareness — vibrating inside my body, mind, and soul.

I experienced indescribable feelings of awe and wonder and total joy as I completely opened myself up and accepted this radiant, vibrant energy of spiritual awareness and enlightenment as it entered inside of me, knowing that it had always been part of me.

This pure white light opened my awareness to my spiritual essence and knowledge. As the light became brighter within me, I became more aware of my inner spiritual knowledge — knowledge that is infinite and goes beyond words or thoughts.

I knew that this light was the light of my soul — the light of the Universe — the light of my spiritual essence vibrating all around me and within me.

This was the light that had shimmered through the mist in the forest and had sparkled with the energy essence of the Universe in the rainbow-colored drops of the waterfall. This was the light that I'd first seen in the rainbow through the open window in my dream.

I heard my rainbow voice talk to me. "Breathe in the light. Become the light and be the light. As you breathe in the pure energy of the light, and fully absorb it within yourself, your spiritual enlightenment completely opens up inside you and you become more aware and awake than ever before.

"As you accept the light that is radiating from within the center of the sunrise, from within the center of your being — your soul — you become fully aware of your true spiritual nature and you know that **you are the universal essence of light that shines upon the Earth.**

"The light within you becomes brighter as the sun continues to rise. Your spiritual knowledge and the awareness of your true nature is interwoven with the rays of sunshine, with the colors of a new day, a new beginning.

"Your inner awareness becomes clearer and brighter at every moment, as you experience and enjoy the sunrise, as you experience enlightenment within your heart, mind, and soul."

I was in complete harmony with the light of the sun and the light of my soul. The light of the sun and the light of my soul were one and the same. I was the essence of light; my soul was composed of the energies of light. I had become the sunrise. I was the sunrise.

I'd found the treasure; it was the treasure of spiritual knowledge — the gift of my spiritual self awakening within me. Having been given this gift, I wanted to share it.

Knowing this, I saw a golden sun ray that emanated and shimmered from the sunrise, a golden sun ray that emanated and radiated from within me. I saw how the sun ray originated from the sun and from me, and how it travels from its source to gently touch the Earth and to light the way of a beautiful new day.

I noticed that this sun ray sparkled on the water and shone on the beach where I had watched the dawn begin, where I'd enjoyed the beginning of the sunrise.

I traveled with the golden sun ray onto the beach where I had watched the sunrise — the dawning of the light within myself, within my soul.

I was now sitting on the beach and I saw that the sun was completely above the horizon, above the clouds. The clouds that had reflected the early colors of dawn and the water that had mirrored the sunrise now reflected the color of gold — the color of the sun and the color of spiritual knowledge.

The sky was a very bright blue and even as I looked at the clouds that were golden, they changed to a pure white as if they'd absorbed the light of the sunrise.

Looking over the water, I noticed how the sunlight sparkles and shimmers, mirroring and reflecting the light from the sun. I knew that the white light of the Universe — the light of my soul — shines and shimmers brightly within me.

I smiled up at the sun, knowing that I'd remembered all the wonderful secrets of my soul and discovered the treasure of my spiritual knowledge on the journey I'd just taken beyond the spectrum of the sunrise, on the rainbow path inside my dream.

Thank you, Rainbow, I whispered, for showing me and reminding me about the true nature of my soul. Thank you for waking me up to my spiritual self.

Ten

Awakening

As I awakened, I looked out the open window and noticed that the sun was well above the horizon, shining brightly. I saw the rainbow sparkling and shimmering with light, vibrating rainbow colors all around me. I heard her whisper to me.

"As you continue to open up and explore your inner knowing, and as you more fully remember and awaken your true spiritual self every day, it's like the dawn of a new beginning that offers a promise of many new and wonderful adventures and discoveries.

"Your remembrance of your inner truth and knowledge, and the awakening of your spiritual self is reflected and mirrored in every experience in your life as you explore this path that you're now traveling — a magical, mystical path — a rainbow path.

"As you continue upon this path, many treasures and rewards open up to you and are offered with every step you take. Spiritual knowledge is the most wonderful treasure of all, because this knowledge leads you to the true awareness of your spirituality and empowers you to express your inner knowing in all your thoughts, feelings, and experiences."

The rainbow shimmered with light again, showering me with awareness. "My sincere wish for you is a lifetime filled with joy and happiness, wonder and awe. Travel lightly on your rainbow path."